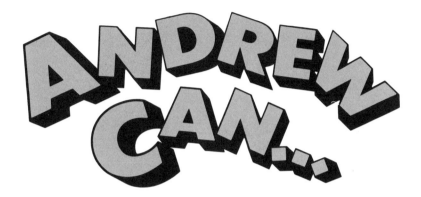

RosAnne Tetz

Pacific Press Publishing Association
Boise, Idaho
Oshawa, Ontario, Canada

Edited by Aileen Andres Sox
Design and cover color by Tim Larson
Cover and interior art by James Converse
Typeset in 14/40 Times Roman

All Scripture quotations come from the International Children's Bible.

Copyright © 1992 by
Pacific Press Publishing Association
Printed in United States of America
All Rights Reserved

ISBN: 0-8163-1063-7

92 93 94 95 96 • 5 4 3 2 1

Andrew

Cassie

Mama

Daddy

Jesus

Grandma

Grandpa

Nina

Alberto

Cousin Matthew

Yogi the dog

Kitty

ANDREW CAN WASH HIS HANDS

"God . . . will make us clean from all the wrongs we have done" (1 John 1:9)

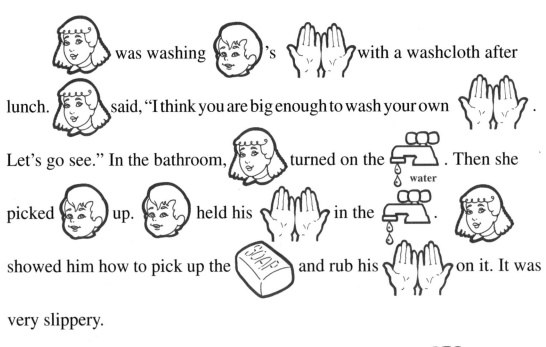

was washing 's with a washcloth after lunch. said, "I think you are big enough to wash your own . Let's go see." In the bathroom, turned on the . Then she picked up. held his in the . showed him how to pick up the and rub his on it. It was very slippery.

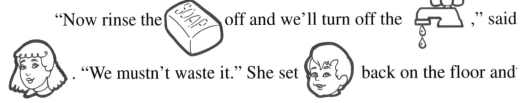

"Now rinse the off and we'll turn off the ," said . "We mustn't waste it." She set back on the floor and gave him a . He patted his dry. "Now your are nice and clean," said . When came home, told him that Andrew was able to wash his now.

"Is that right?" said. "You don't look tall enough to reach the . I have a good idea." went down to the basement. He got a stool. "Come stand on this, buddy," he said. "This will make you taller."

When stood on the stool, he could reach the and the and even the . He washed his for supper. At the table bowed his head and said, "Dear , thank You for this food and thank You that is learning so many things. Amen."

ANDREW CAN GIVE

"Give, and you will receive" (Luke 6:38).

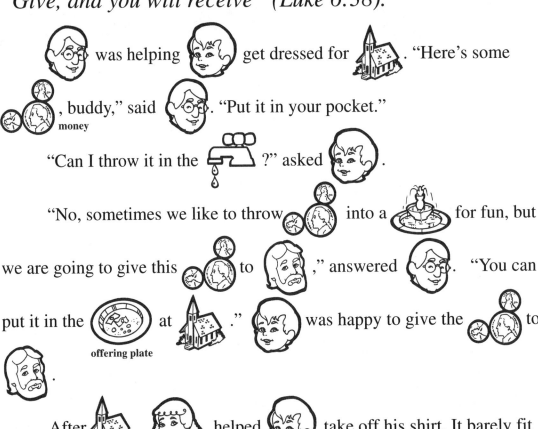

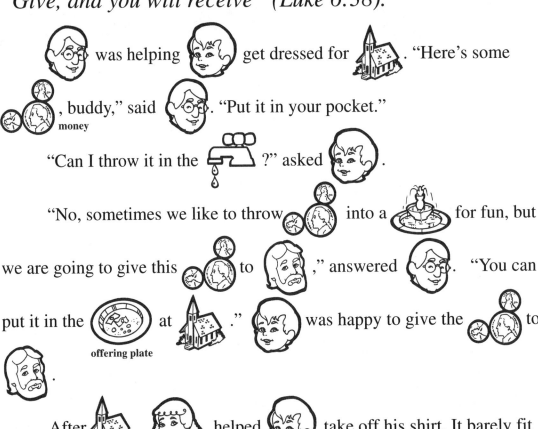 was helping 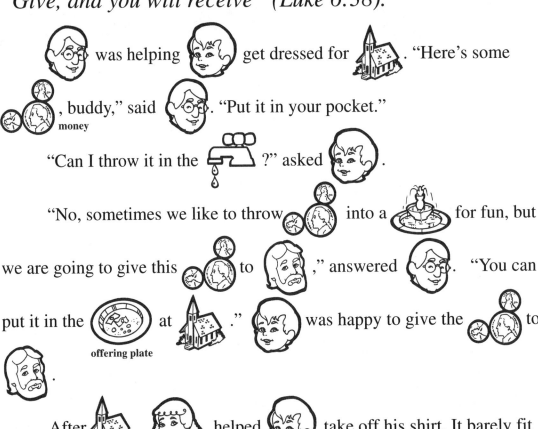 get dressed for . "Here's some

, buddy," said . "Put it in your pocket."
money

"Can I throw it in the ?" asked .

"No, sometimes we like to throw into a for fun, but

we are going to give this to ," answered . "You can

put it in the at ." was happy to give the to
offering plate

.

After , helped take off his shirt. It barely fit

over his head. ", you are getting so big," said . "This shirt

doesn't fit you anymore."

"Give it to  ," said  .

"Good idea," agreed  . "We give lots of your clothes to  . But I think a little boy would like this shirt better. Shall we give it to  's baby brother?"

 reached into the closet. "Here is the picture you painted and the  you picked out for  's birthday," she said. "Shall we go have a happy-birthday lunch now?"  grabbed the  and ran to the kitchen.

"Happy birthday,  !"  shouted, and he gave  a big hug and a kiss. "I helped make you a  ."

"Oh, boy!" said  . "Thank you for giving me a very happy birthday."

ANDREW CAN SAY "PLEASE"

"Ask, and God will give to you" (Matthew 7:7).

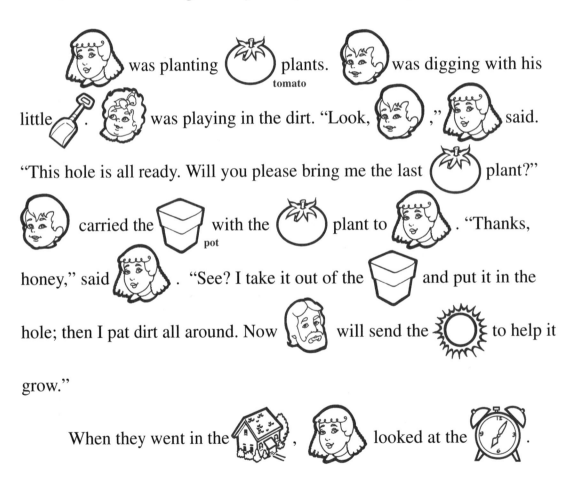

was planting tomato plants. was digging with his little . was playing in the dirt. "Look, ," said. "This hole is all ready. Will you please bring me the last plant?"

carried the pot with the plant to . "Thanks, honey," said . "See? I take it out of the and put it in the hole; then I pat dirt all around. Now will send the to help it grow."

When they went in the , looked at the .

8

"Oh, it's very late, and we're very dirty. Let's call 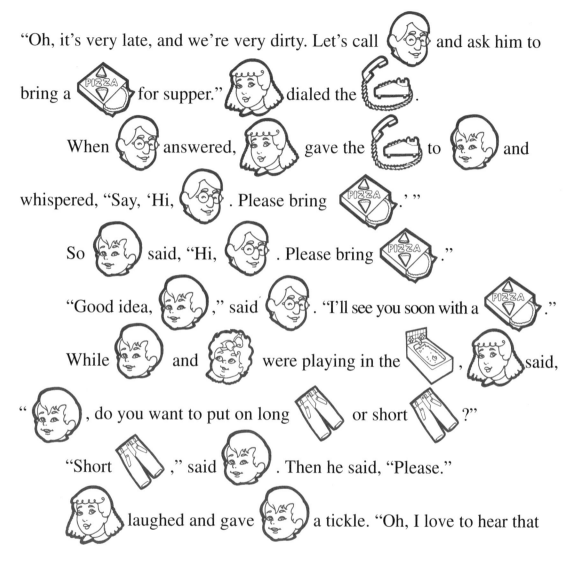 and ask him to bring a PIZZA for supper." dialed the .

When answered, gave the to and whispered, "Say, 'Hi, . Please bring PIZZA.' "

So said, "Hi, . Please bring PIZZA."

"Good idea, ," said . "I'll see you soon with a PIZZA."

While and were playing in the , said,

" , do you want to put on long or short ?"

"Short ," said . Then he said, "Please."

laughed and gave a tickle. "Oh, I love to hear that word. When you say Please, it makes me very happy."

ANDREW CAN KEEP TRYING

"Never give up" (Ephesians 6:18).

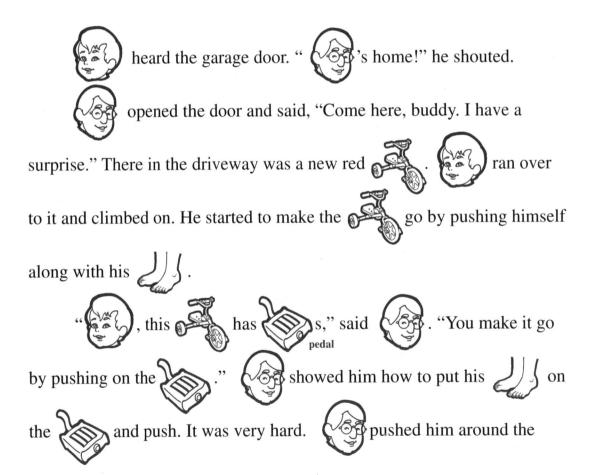 heard the garage door. " 's home!" he shouted.

opened the door and said, "Come here, buddy. I have a surprise." There in the driveway was a new red . ran over to it and climbed on. He started to make the go by pushing himself along with his .

" , this has s," said . "You make it go by pushing on the ." showed him how to put his on the and push. It was very hard. pushed him around the

10

driveway so he could feel how the  went up and down.

tried again to push the  by himself. It was very hard. "We'll try

some more after supper," said . "Let's go eat."

After supper, tried and tried to push the . Finally,

 said, "It's bedtime, sweetheart. You can try some more tomorrow."

When he was all tucked in, helped thank 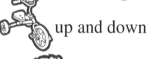 for his

new .

The next day, practiced and practiced. By the time

came home from work, was riding his new up and down

the driveway. After supper the family went for a walk. rode in her

, but rode his .

ANDREW CAN BE GENTLE

"Be gentle and polite to all people" (Titus 3:2).

and his family went to ___'s ___ to have a picnic in the backyard. ___ and ___ played on her ___ set and chased each other in the grass. ___'s ___ watched everything from the steps. ___ picked up a ___ (stick) and started waving it around. ___ ran away. ___ looked surprised. "___, ___ is afraid of you when you wave the ___ like that," said ___. "You must be very gentle around ___. You are so big, and she is so little." ___ put the ___ down so ___ wouldn't be afraid to come back.

and saw a . They tiptoed over to look at it,

but it flew away. "Why did it fly away, ?" asked .

"Wild s are afraid of people, even gentle people," said

. "When comes, He will fix everything so the s won't

be afraid of us anymore."

When they got home, was happy to see them. He ran around

to welcome everyone home. 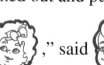 was sitting on the floor. When

ran up to see her, she reached out and pulled his ears. Poor yipped

and jumped away. "No, 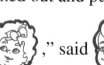," said . "Be gentle." Then he gave

 a nice, soft pat to show her how.

13

ANDREW CAN WAIT

"Wait and trust the Lord" (Psalm 37:7).

 put down the . " is coming to see me," he

said. "Let's go to the airport."

"Not yet," said 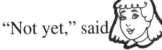 . "We have to wait a few days until we go to

 and then wait a few more days after that."

After   said, "Can we get ?"

"Not yet," said , "but after our nap we can take to the

park."

The next day asked, "How long until  comes?"

 said, "We must wait three more days. Would you like to see

if can come play with us today?"

14

The next day, when 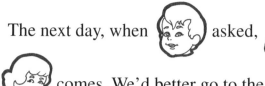 asked, said, "It's two more days

until comes. We'd better go to the grocery store today."

The next morning said, "Only one more day!"

Early the next morning climbed onto his parents' big .

"Wake up," he said, "let's go get ."

"We've got to get dressed first," said . "We can't go to the

airport in our pajamas!"

"And we'll have to eat breakfast and brush our teeth and feed ,"

said . "Then we can go."

At the airport, watched the s come and go. He waited

at the gate while lots of people walked by. Finally he saw .

"Hi, ," he shouted. "I've been waiting for you!"

ANDREW CAN TRUST

"So, trust the Lord always" (Isaiah 26:4).

was playing in the big swimming pool. was bouncing in the shallow , but had on his wings so he could play with in the deep . twirled him around like an . Then pretended he was an , and he chased

alligator

around in the .

said, "Look at the big boys jumping into the pool."

"They are jumping off the ," said . "Would you like to do that someday?"

"Yes," said .

"Then let's practice," said . "Come to the side of the pool."

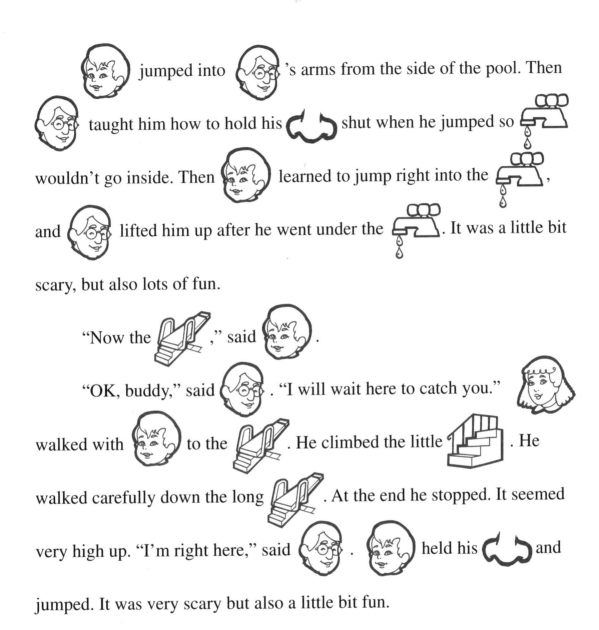

jumped into 's arms from the side of the pool. Then taught him how to hold his shut when he jumped so wouldn't go inside. Then learned to jump right into the , and lifted him up after he went under the . It was a little bit scary, but also lots of fun.

"Now the ," said .

"OK, buddy," said . "I will wait here to catch you."

walked with to the . He climbed the little . He walked carefully down the long . At the end he stopped. It seemed very high up. "I'm right here," said . held his and jumped. It was very scary but also a little bit fun.

ANDREW CAN BE A GOOD EXAMPLE

"Be careful. Don't think these little children are worth nothing"
(Matthew 18:10).

was eating supper. "I want more   ," he said, and he banged his   on the   .   banged her   on her   .

"   , don't bang your   ," said   . "And when you want something, say Please."   stopped banging. He said Please.

"Have some   ," said   .
green beans

"I don't want   ," said   , and he pushed his   away.   pushed her   away too.
plate

"Well, you need to eat some anyway," said   .

18

" , look," said . " is a copycat. Whatever you do, she tries to do too."

"She copies me," said .

"You must be careful," said . "When you do something bad, will try to do it too. But if you do something good, she will try to be like you."

"I don't want her to copy me," said .

"Sorry, buddy," said . "That's part of being a big brother."

"Try doing something good," said . "See if she will copy it."

 ate some  . So did .

"She did it!" laughed. So did .

19

ANDREW CAN HELP

"Whatever work you do, do your best" (Ecclesiastes 9:5).

One morning [Andrew] was playing with his [airplane].

[Mother] rocked [baby] in the [rocking chair]. "[Andrew]," [Mother] called. "Would you please bring me [baby]'s [blanket]? I think she is cold."

blanket

[Andrew] jumped up and ran to the nursery. He found the [blanket] and

took it to [Mother]. "Thank you, sweetheart," [Mother] said. "You are my

big helper." And she gave him a kiss.

In the afternoon [baby] was sitting in her [swing]. All of her [toys]

toys

had fallen on the floor. She looked like she might cry.

[Andrew] picked up her [rubber duck] and gave it to her. [baby] laughed

rubber duck

20

and started to chew on the 's head. smiled at her big brother.

In the evening and were playing horsie. Then said, "It's almost time, . Let's pick up the now."

helped put his in the bucket. "It makes happy when

blocks

you help," said . "It makes me happy too. Here is a hug for my best

boy."

ANDREW CAN OBEY

Lord, "help me obey . . . because that makes me happy"
(Psalm 119:35).

 went to the zoo with , , and .

rode in her , but could walk.

First they visited the s. The s jumped and chased and

played. laughed. They were so funny. "Come on, ,"

said. "Let's go see more animals." came running. gave

him a little hug.

Then they went to see the . The were lazy. They

just lay in the grass, sleeping. started to climb on the rail so he

could see better. "Come here, ," said . "It's not safe to

22

climb there." 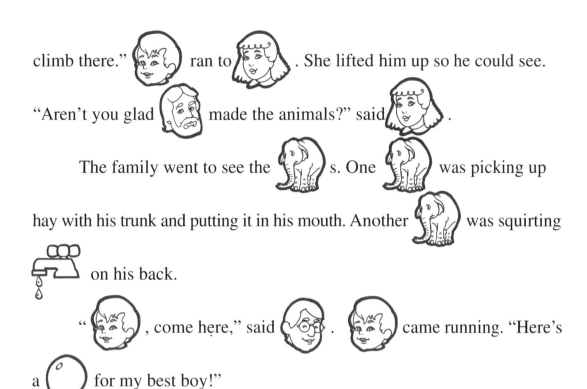 ran to . She lifted him up so he could see.

"Aren't you glad made the animals?" said .

The family went to see the s. One was picking up

hay with his trunk and putting it in his mouth. Another was squirting

on his back.

" , come here," said . came running. "Here's

a for my best boy!"

balloon

23

ANDREW CAN LISTEN

"The Lord God . . . teaches me to listen" (Isaiah 50:4).

, , and decided to go for a walk. got

out the . ran to find the leash so could come too.

They had just started walking when stopped. "Listen, ,"

she said. "What's that noise?"

 listened carefully. "A !" he said.

"That's right," said . "Maybe it is saying thank you to

for such a pretty day."

After a few minutes,  pushed the to the very edge of

the road. "Listen, ," she said. "What's that noise?"

listened. "A !" he said.

"Yes, we must be careful," said , pulling over to the

grass while the  drove by.

Soon they had walked around the block. As was lifting

 from the , she said, "Listen, , what's that noise?"

 listened. "The 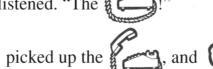!"

 picked up the , and said, "Hello, is

there?"

 put the  by his ear. said, "Hello, . I

love you!"

ANDREW CAN SHARE

"They shared everything" (Acts 2:44)

's friend had come to play. wanted to play with 's toy . grabbed the away from him. began to cry. " just wants a turn to play," said. "He won't keep your . Can you share?" put the back in 's . He began to build a garage with his .

watched the boys as they played. She laughed every time the fell over. lay on her tummy by the . "Let's see if is big enough to knock over the ," said . She stacked three  up.  waved her around and knocked

the  down. and began to stack for  .

Everyone laughed and played and had fun together.

After lunch the boys threw some leftover crumbs on the

porch for the s to eat. said, "I am so glad gave us

each other so we could share our fun. You have been good sharers today.

You shared your with each other and with  . You even

shared your with your animal friends."

ANDREW CAN LAUGH

"You will laugh with joy" (Luke 6:21).

 was watching play the game with .

 held 's hand closed. "Here is the ," said .

"But where are the ?"

 wiggled all his fingers in front of . "Here they are!"

he laughed.

"You silly!" grabbed and gave him a big tickle. "You

are supposed to wait until we count them in the poem." and

and had a big roll-around hug on the rug.

 came in to see what all the laughing was about. "Is there

anybody here who would like a ?" asked.

28

"Yes,"  said, " and I are going to make a ." and put between them and gave a big squeeze. "!" they yelled.

"That looks good," said. "I want to make one too." So and squeezed both kids between them. "Kid !" everyone yelled.

Then they all went into the kitchen to help make es.

spread peanut butter on his bread, and then he put raisins on it to make a funny face. When they sat down to eat, prayed, "Dear ,

Thank You for this food and thank You for our fun day. Amen."

And said Amen too.

ANDREW CAN SLEEP

"I go to bed and sleep in peace" (Psalm 4:8).

It was very late, but could not go to sleep. had read him some stories. had gotten him a drink of . They had given him good-night kisses, and he had his to hold. But he could

piggy

not go to sleep. " ," he called. When came in, said, "I'm not sleepy." picked him up and sat in the . She cuddled him and rocked him and sang him a song.

came in. "It's your turn," said .

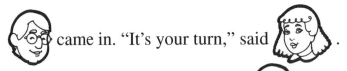

"Can't you sleep, buddy?" asked as he sat down in the

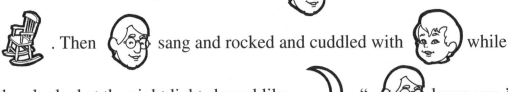

. Then sang and rocked and cuddled with while they looked at the night light shaped like a . " loves you,"

30

whispered. "And loves you. And loves you." began to name all the people who knew . " and love you. loves you. loves you." named many, many people.

listened and listened. He liked this story very much. " loves you," said . "And 's loves you, and loves you even more." The went *squeak, creak, squeak, creak.* "But most of all," whispered , " loves you. loves you most of all."

" loves me," said in a very sleepy voice. "And I love ." Then put him in his with his again, and this time went to sleep.

Dedicated to Andrew

and Cassie